What'

Adults think they can get away with anything just because they're big and loud and have got more cash than us ... but they can't! And this book has all the best schemes in the world for pulling the wool over grown-ups' eyes. Whether it's dodging dinner-time duties, or a scam for staying up late, we'll provide the best excuses yet and what's more, our methods are so foolproof that the poor old grown-ups won't even know they've been had ... until it's too late!

Also by Jim and Duncan Eldridge in Red Fox

How to Handle Grown-ups
More Ways to Handle Grown-ups
What Grown-ups Say and What They Really Mean
The Complete How to Handle Grown-ups
Bogeys, Boils and Belly Buttons

EVEN MORE WAYS TO HANDLE GROWN-UPS

Jim and Duncan Eldridge
Illustrated by Harry Venning

RED FOX

A Red Fox Book

Published by Random House Children's Books
20 Vauxhall Bridge Road, London SW1V 2SA

A division of Random House UK Ltd
London Melbourne Sydney Auckland
Johannesburg and agencies throughout the world

1 3 5 7 9 10 8 6 4 2

First published by Red Fox 1996

Printed and bound in Great Britain by
Cox and Wyman Ltd, Reading, Berkshire

Papers used by Random House UK Ltd are natural, recyclable products made from wood grown in sustainable forests. The manufacturing processes conform to the environmental regulations of the country of origin.

RANDOM HOUSE UK Limited Reg. No. 954009

ISBN 0 09 953031 7

Contents

Part One: At Home

Part Two: At School

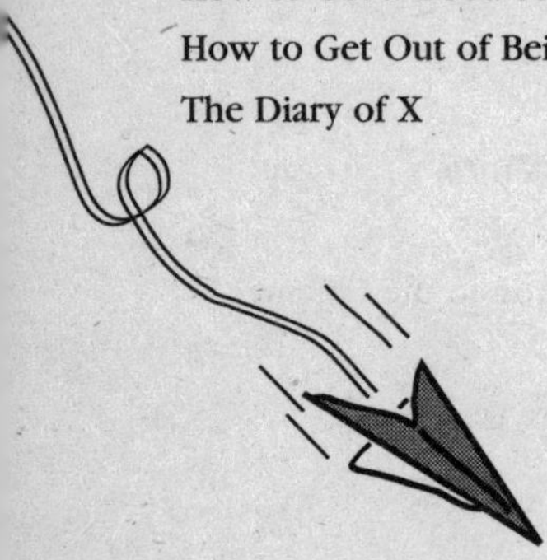

PART ONE: AT HOME

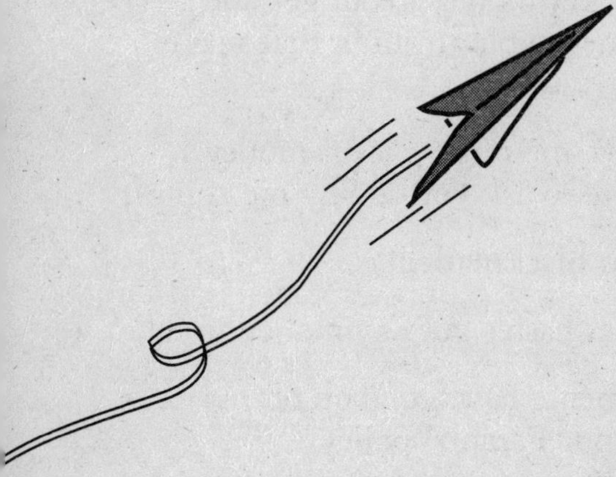

How to Get More Pocket Money

They're doing a survey at school on how much pocket money we all get and I don't want people to think that you're mean.

If you give me more pocket money I won't have to ask you to buy me things.

I'm being blackmailed!

My pocket hasn't got any money in it.

The payments have gone up on my 'Insure Your Parents' policy.

The weight of all these coins is making holes in my pockets, so I reckon paper money will save the wear and tear on my clothes.

The more money I have, the easier it'll be for me to learn to be financially independent.

Inflation has cut the value of my pocket money to zilch.

This paper says that the sooner children learn to handle their own money the better it is for their parents.

Have you got change for a pound? Thanks! I'll give you the pound later.

I'm collecting for the M.Y.S.E.L.F. charity. Would you like to donate?

I need some money to buy some books/ pens/pencils/writing paper (anything that sounds like it's for school).

If you give me some money I can get your shopping for you.

I want to open a Saving/Investing/ Spending Account.

Granny says, 'Money is the root of all evil,' so if you give yours to me I'll throw it away for you.

You're always saying you're worried about money, so why don't you let me have some and I'll share your burden.

The local newspaper is publishing a list of poor children and I'm going to be one of them.

The TV said that using cash instead of credit cards is causing adults stress, so I'll help you by using your cash for you.

Excuses for Not Having Done the Washing Up/Washed

My teacher says our water's polluted and if I washed/washed up I'd spread that pollution onto us.

There's something moving in the water!

I thought we'd save money on the water rates, so I'm waiting for it to rain.

Great! I can try out this new plate juggling act I saw on the telly.

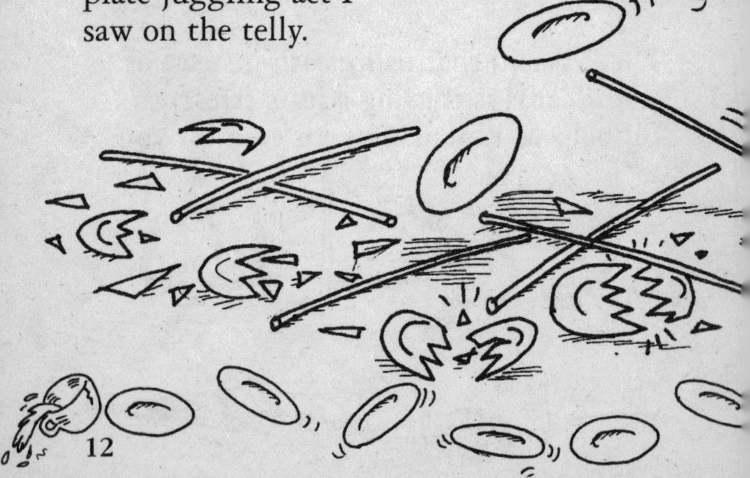

I put all the dishes in to soak and I'm waiting for the 'grease and grime to just float off' like it does in the advert.

I'm afraid I can't wash up because it's against my religion.

I can't wash up with this liquid because it's bad for the environment.

I thought you wanted to have a bath/shower and I didn't want to use up all the hot water.

Excuses for Having Broken Crockery

I was trying to be helpful and put them away.

I thought it was a Virtual Reality cup.

They shouldn't sell plates that break that easily, they're a hazard to health and safety.

It had a crack in it and I was worried that if I left it like that germs would gather in the crack and anyone who used it would get seriously ill.

I thought you said you hated it and wanted to get rid of it, so I did it for you.

My teacher says crockery is unhygienic and that if we're going to stay healthy we should all use paper plates and cups.

HOW TO GET YOUR GROWN-UP TO BUY YOU SOMETHING

There's a competition in the paper for The Most Generous Person and I'd like to put your name forward for it.

Knowing how to work this computer program is essential if I'm to get a job when I leave school.

What does 'deprived' mean? I only ask because that's what they're calling me at school.

Everyone in the whole school has got one of those (whatever it is) except me!

I'd like that so I'll always be reminded of what a wonderful parent/aunt/uncle you are.

The paper says the price of that is going to double next week, so you'd better get me one now while you can still afford it!

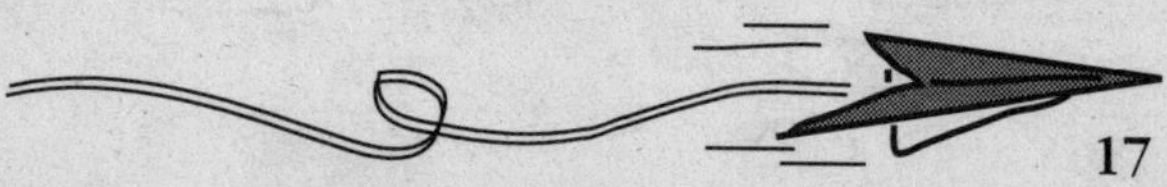

EXCUSES FOR NOT EATING CERTAIN FOODS

I can't eat that potato/chop/carrot. It looks just like my best friend.

I read in the paper that they make this from stray cats and dogs they catch in the street.

I've got to walk/run/ride/play a video game after dinner and all that food will give me indigestion.

I've got to stick to 200 calories a day. I've already had 170 and that looks like a lot more than 30 to me.

I'm on hunger strike till I get more pocket money.

This is made artificially by genetic engineering. If I eat it I'll turn into some sort of monster, like a cross between a plant and an animal.

How to Get More Food

There's no room in the fridge to keep left-overs, so we'd better eat it all now.

This is nearly past its sell-by date, so I'd better eat it before it goes off.

A teacher at school said I looked malnourished.

The canteen staff at school are on strike, so I need to take a big packed lunch with me.

People have been making fun of me and calling me Skinny.

This is the best meal I've ever had in my whole life! I could eat it all over again!

I've got a parasite living in my stomach that eats half of everything I eat.

The fridge has broken down! I'd better eat everything before it goes rotten and has to be thrown away.

Excuses for Watching TV

I'm seeing if I can hypnotise myself with it.

I want to be a TV director when I grow up so I'm learning how it's done.

I'm sure this programme was made in our town. I'm watching out for anyone I know in the background.

This is an interactive programme and by watching it I'm playing my part in the development of new technology.

It's important that I keep up with current affairs and TV is the most instant form of media.

The optician said this is the best kind of exercise for my eyes.

I'm seeing if I can change channels by thought power.

I'm learning how to use a remote control so I can get a hi-tech job when I grow up.

Excuses for Not Doing the Shopping

The Child Cruelty people are keeping a watch on the shopping centre to see which children in this area are being used as slaves.

I might catch a computer virus from the bar codes.

The school bully says he's going to get me and he hangs around by the shops.

Someone told me the shopping centre is actually an alien spacecraft. People going into it have disappeared and never been seen again.

I can't work out how much change I should get without my computer, and I can't take it with me.

Why don't we do our shopping by phone like modern people?

Excuses for Having Torn / Soaked / Damaged Clothes

I was doing a bungee jump and the elastic broke.

This isn't my coat.

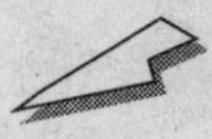

My clothes are dirty because I'm doing the 'before' part of an advert for a new soap powder.

Torn clothing is all the rage these days – it's called the distressed look.

It's a hologram of a tear, I got it from a joke shop.

On my way home I had to rescue this lady's poodle that had fallen into a swamp/rubbish bin/manhole.

I've been doing my part to save the Environment by helping recycle waste from the local rubbish tip.

This is my costume for the school play. I've got the part of Oliver Twist.

How to Get Out of Doing Household Chores

I thought you liked looking after me?

I've got a blister on my thumb.

I'm waiting for us to get a machine to do these jobs.

My PE teacher says I've got to take it easy for a while.

This is child slavery!

Promise you won't get upset if I break anything?

I saw on the TV that children forced to work often become criminals when they grow up.

I'd love to, but I'm afraid I've got lots of homework to do.

Excuses for Not Having Bought a Birthday Card / Present

I read in the paper that they were changing the calendar to make the year shorter and your birthday was one of the days that was being cut out.

I sent you your birthday greetings on the internet. As soon as you buy a computer with a modem you'll be able to get it.

I thought the best thing I could give you was my happiness, so I spent the money for your present on me instead.

I thought you wanted your birthday kept a secret.

I didn't want to remind you that you were one year nearer to dying of old age.

There was nothing in any of the shops that was worthy of you.

Here it is – your Virtual Reality birthday card... Drat, it's vanished again!

It was so big I had to leave it outside the house and someone must have stolen it during the night.

It was in this box. It must have escaped.

Excuses for Not Going to School

The heating system packed up today and we've been told to stay away for three days while they repair it.

Because our school is short of teachers it's going over to a new system where we all only do two days a week at school, and three days at home.

Our school has got a new system so we can work at home using a modem connecting our computers to the school's computer.

The car alarm/dog/gale/thunder and lightning kept me awake all night and I'm too exhausted to go.

I was up all night doing my homework.

There's a pupils' strike on.

I can't go to school today because I'm doing some voluntary work for charity.

I'm doing a sponsored lie-in for world peace.

Excuses for Staying Up Late

I heard a strange noise in my room.

The TV went wrong at eleven o'clock last night, I want to see if it happens again.

I can't go to bed yet, I'm nearly on Level two (or three or four or five) of this game!

I've got to stay up and do this homework.

I've just eaten some cheese – if I go to bed now I'll have a nightmare!

Patrick Moore said that there's going to be a partial eclipse of the moon at one o'clock in the morning and I was sure you'd want to see it.

I'm doing a research project on nocturnal animals.

Human beings waste too much time sleeping.

I'm doing an experiment to see how long I can go without sleep.

I think I've got insomnia.

My bed's uncomfortable so I'm going to wait till I'm really tired before I lie on it.

The Open University's on telly later and it's about a subject I'm doing my school project on!

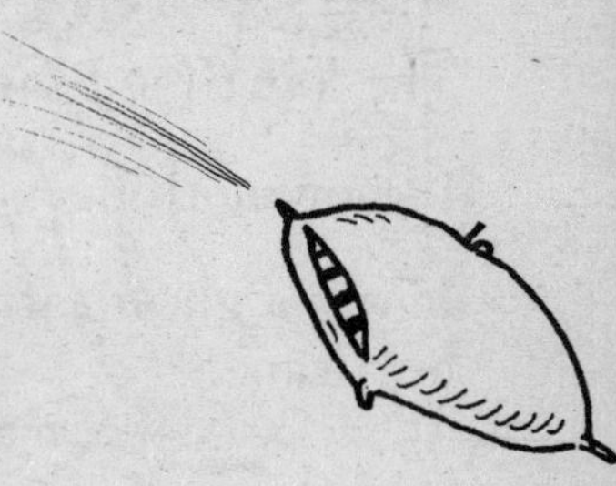

EXCUSES FOR HAVING BROKEN / DAMAGED / TORN HOUSEHOLD OBJECTS

I was trying to save a mouse/bird/tortoise/elephant that was trapped in it.

I came home and found a burglar in here! I was rushing at him when he threw it at me and it broke.

The computer did it.

It was part of a 'Deconstruction' project I'm doing.

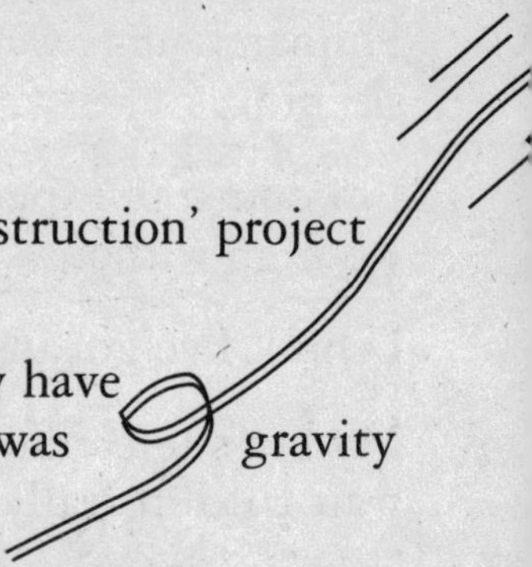

It's not my fault! I may have knocked it over but it was gravity that made it fall down!

The last time I saw it, it was in one piece.

I know nothing!

It was a ghost/earthquake/flood/hurricane.

I think I've spotted a design fault. I think I should get paid by the British Safety Standards people.

They warned people about that on *Watchdog*.

I was practising for *Gladiators*.

How To Get Your Grown-up To Take You To The Cinema / Fair / For A Meal

There's a special offer this week while this film's on: free popcorn!

This film is of a book we're doing at school and our teacher says we've got to see it.

It's not healthy to stay indoors all the time!

Mum/Dad, don't you feel like a prisoner within your own home?

Apparently adults get in free if accompanied by a child.

Did your parents never take you out when you were a child?

How to Get Out Of Going Somewhere (e.g. Visiting Relatives)

You didn't hear the terrible things Gran/Uncle/Aunt said about you last time, while you were out of the room.

A man dropped dead with bubonic plague last week at that museum/art gallery/park.

On the weather forecast they advised all motorists and pedestrians to stay at home.

If we were on the Internet we could do it all from home and we wouldn't have to waste time travelling.

You're always saying we haven't got any money so let's save the fare by not going.

I don't like going to their house because their children are a bad influence on me.

Excuses for Why Video Games Are Good for You

If I can learn to handle Virtual Reality then I'll be able to cope more easily with real life.

Our teacher says they're the best way to learn about computers.

They keep me occupied so I won't be in your way.

I've found out that the games in the arcade are linked to the electricity supply in our house, so if I play games there I can divert our electricity charges to them and save you pounds!

This optician on TV said that video games are the best exercise for your eyes.

I'm learning to live in the Virtual Reality world where we'll all be living in a few year's time, so I'm actually preparing for the future.

How to Get Your Grown-Up to Take You Away on Holiday

You (that is, your grown-up) deserve a good holiday after working hard all year.

If you take me I can do things like test that the water isn't too cold before you go in the sea.

Travel is good for my education.

The whole of this area is due to be struck by locusts/plague the first two weeks in August.

There's going to be a new hole in the ozone layer this summer – right above our house!

A holiday abroad will help me improve my Spanish/Greek/Italian/Tibetan.

How to Get Out Of Looking After Small Brothers/Sisters/Pets

It's unfair to give me the 'life or death' responsibility for another living creature.

I'm sure I saw the dog/cat/budgie/little brother foaming at the mouth – it might be rabies.

I don't believe in imprisoning pets, all animals should be allowed to roam free.

Did you hear about the last time I looked after someone's pet – the RSPCA didn't find it until four weeks later.

Of course I don't mind, so long as your pet doesn't mind the fact that I've got fleas.

How to Get Out of Hanging Out Washing

They're not all my clothes.

If I run out of clothes pegs can I use a stapler instead?

Are we too poor to afford a dryer?

If I hang those outside all the pollution in the air will make them dirty again.

It looks like rain.

I can't hang them out as it will cast a shadow on the lawn and stunt the growth of the grass.

How to Get Out of Cleaning Up Your Room

All those things are my happy memories – you wouldn't want me to shut them away would you?!

There's a huge spider/rat/germ lurking under my bed and

I daren't disturb it in case it attacks me.

All that clutter isn't really there - it's a Virtual Reality program I made up on my computer, and I can't switch it off or I'll lose the program.

It may look like mess to you, but to me it's a three-dimensional sculpture.

I've arranged my room according to chaos theory.

It's part of a biology project I'm doing (this can apply to just about anything with mould on it).

I'm making a personal statement about clutter.

The police told me not to touch anything in this room until they get here.

I've got a good system going here – if I tidy up I won't be able to find anything.

PART TWO: AT SCHOOL

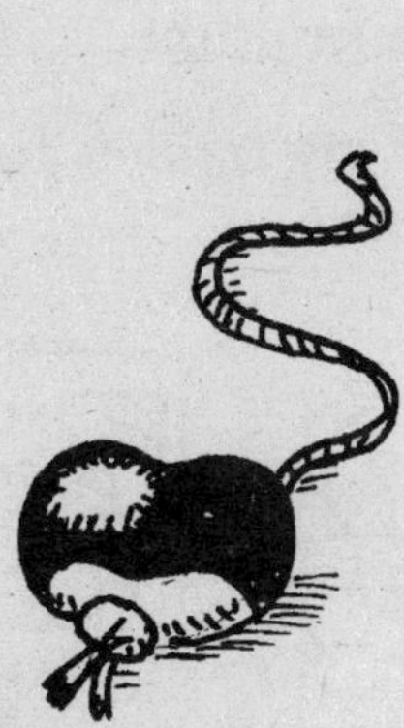

I thought the school was closed today for voting.

My dad bought a new alarm clock yesterday and we found out this morning it's set to Japanese time.

One of my trainers had a puncture.

The bus had to take a detour via Birmingham/Glasgow/Timbuktu to avoid road works.

I had to cook breakfast for my entire family.

A UFO beamed me up, took me to the Planet Zod, then bought me back here – late!

I thought the clocks had gone back.

I got lost.

I forgot where the school was.

For my Geography project I was making a map of How To Get To School so that new pupils, who live in my area, can find their way to school easily and it took me longer than I thought to write down all the street names on the way.

I had to wait until the school crossing patrol man/woman arrived before I could cross the road, and he/she was late.

I'm not late for today, I'm early for tomorrow.

Excuses for Not Handing In Homework

I thought you meant next Tuesday.

I did it on my computer at home and kept it on the disk, but my brother wiped it.

I had to save the world from destruction last night.

I've done it and it's in my head – I want to see if I can communicate it to you by telepathy.

Aliens zapped it out of my hand as I was bringing it to school.

I did it on my computer but, before I could save it, it crashed.

I saw on the news that the United Nations have banned all children from working, so I thought that meant working after school on things like homework as well.

I can't do homework because my body clock switches the thinking part of my brain off at 4 o'clock in the afternoon.

Our whole family lives in one tiny cupboard so there's nowhere for me to work.

Our family does everything in body language instead of writing, so I was going to act out my Maths homework for you in mime.

How to Get Out of Lessons

GENERAL

I've got flu/measles/plague and I'm not allowed to sit with other people.

I've got a phobia about being in enclosed spaces.

Where's the nearest fire extinguisher in case I spontaneously combust – it's happened to me four times already!

ENGLISH

My dad/mum says that as I can already speak it, I don't need to learn it.

My dad/mum says that it's not worth studying English because it's a dying language. He/she says we should all be learning Chinese.

MATHS

My religion forbids me to study anything that doesn't praise it.

Because of a space-time accident I can now only do fourth-dimensional Maths.

SCIENCE

I've got to stay here and look after my friend who became invisible because of last week's Science experiment.

After seeing that film *The Fly* my parents have banned me from all Science lessons in case the same thing happens to me.

SOCIAL STUDIES

I'm not allowed to do History because my dad/mum says it's all political propaganda and they don't want me to be brainwashed.

Because the world changes so fast anything we study today won't be relevant tomorrow, so what's the point?

MUSIC

I'm not allowed to use musical instruments that other people have touched in case I pick up their germs.

Because all music is now computer-generated my parents say I can do it at home using my modem.

This is my new composition called 'Silence'.

How To Get Out Of Working In Lessons

My optician says I mustn't use my eyes in case I strain them before my eye test next week.

My pen won't work.

I've left my brain to medical science and the hospital have told me I mustn't use it any more.

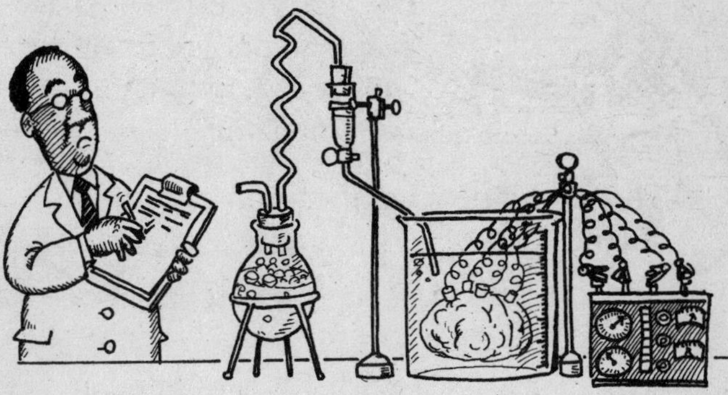

How to Get Picked For the School Team

Wow, Sir/Miss, I wish I was as good at sports as you! You're my hero!

I don't like to be a sneak, Sir/Miss, but (name of person you hate who always gets picked for the team) told a friend of mine that you have to pick him/her because he/she is blackmailing you, which is why there's never any room left on the team for me!

I don't really want people to know my mum/dad's a famous athlete because I want to be successful in my own right.

How to Get Out of Doing Sports

I've sprained my ankle/knee/wrist/elbow/head.

My doctor says I mustn't go out in this bad weather in case I get pneumonia.

My doctor says I mustn't go out in this hot weather in case I get sunstroke.

My religion forbids me to take part in competitive events.

What am I supposed to do with this round object again?

I need to conserve my energy for saving the world from destruction.

I think I've got the rules of this game ... whenever anyone else has got the ball I kick them as hard as I can, right?

Is the school insured in case I get injured?

I'm really not keen on this running bit – couldn't I just stroll leisurely instead?

How to Get the Star Part in the School Play

My dad/mum is a top TV director and they're talking about filming the school play for TV, providing I have a big part in it.

I've always wanted to get the starring role in a play with a great director like Francis Ford Coppola or Martin Scorsese or ... you.

How to Get Out of the School Play

I keep forgetting my line.

But Robert De Niro says those rude words when he's acting!

Yes, but what's my motivation for this part?

I don't believe in rehearsing lines, I just say whatever comes into my head.

What's acting then?

You'll have to talk to my agent.

I'm afraid I've already got a major part acting on the stage of life!

HOW TO GET A GOOD SCHOOL REPORT

My dad says he'll give a Mercedes to the teacher who gives me the best report.

I overheard my parents saying that if I don't get a good school report I'm going to be sold to a family in Antarctica.

I've never had a good school report in my life – if someone was kind and wonderful enough to give me one I'd be their fan for ever and never be trouble in class again.

How to Get Out of Being Punished

My psychiatrist says I'm vulnerable and mustn't suffer unnecessary stress.

My uncle works for Amnesty International and has asked me to give him a report on punishment in this school.

This psychologist said the other day that people who punish other people are just showing how inferior they feel inside.

My dad's seven feet tall and a black belt in karate and he says he doesn't like adults who punish small kids.

The last teacher who punished me disappeared under mysterious circumstances.

Putting it into practice with...

THE DIARY OF X!

Tuesday 2nd

Today has been the worst day in my Entire Life! One bad thing after another kept happening – in fact there were so many bad things that I'm surprised I got off without being struck by lightning and being drowned by a plague of frogs and boils.

The first bad thing was being removed from my starring role in the school play. I was in the middle of my big speech at rehearsal when Miss Potting, the Drama teacher, ordered me off the stage and put that spotty-faced idiot Jim Spinks in my place – and all because she claims I was messing about! I wasn't, it was just that the part, as scripted, that I was playing, was so boring that I did what any proper actor should do and improvised, with the result that I have been substituted by said Gormless Spinks and reduced to the position of Person Who Pulls The Curtains.

What makes it worse is that I had a bet on with Amanda Lucey that, out of the two of us, I would get a bigger round of applause than her! The chances of me getting any applause at all, have now been greatly reduced, so much so that I pointed out to Amanda that with me no longer in the cast it was only fair that our bet should be declared null and void. Instead of agreeing to this like any fair-minded human being, this alien from the Planet Slime insisted the bet still stands and if I don't pay up she'll tell everyone I'm a cheat and a crook. To be honest, I don't care what she says about me, it's just that

I hate getting so obviously beaten by this Amanda ghoul-in-human-shape. I shall now set my brain to work to persuade Miss Potting to either: a) let me back in the play, or b) get Amanda Lucey sacked from it.

The second disastrous thing that happened was that when I got home I was informed by Dad and Mum that they have booked us on an Educational Holiday looking at Roman remains! Aaargh!! I was looking forward to going somewhere with some sun and sand and sea and an arcade with loads of great video games, and instead I'm going to be dragged around some wet and boring city looking at lumps of rock! In my opinion this is cruelty! I considered writing to the Court of European Rights complaining about both my parents and Miss Potting, but thought about it and realized it would be a waste of a stamp. I shall just have to take matters into my own hands and get these people round to my way of thinking.

Wednesday 3rd

Operation Save My Holiday swung into action today. At school I found a video tape all about some horrible disease that eats your flesh and makes bits of you fall

off. I then found another tape about Roman remains in Britain. By editing both tapes together, I was able to make a really horrible tape that suggested that in all the Roman ruins in Britain there lurks this dreaded virus that is just waiting to jump out on innocent passers-by and start eating them alive from the feet upwards.

I took this video home and told my mum and dad I'd found a video in the school library all about Roman remains. Mum and Dad got all happy and Dad patted me on the head and they both said how pleased they were that I was entering into the spirit of things and not sulking because they knew I wanted to go on holiday by the sea and have fun etc etc etc. We all then sat down to watch the video. It was brilliant. They both sat there, smiling and nodding and saying how wonderful it all looked and how they were looking forward to picking up some useless bit of floor tile, when suddenly the virus bits started appearing and bits of flesh started to peel off and they both started to look a bit green. After they'd taken in two decomposing bodies, caused (apparently) by a rogue Roman virus that had lain dormant for thousands of years, Mum switched the tape off and said, 'Maybe we ought to check ahead at each site first.' And Dad nodded. Round one to me. I shall keep up the attack, however, as you should never underestimate your grown-up, they are liable to do the most stupid thing when you least expect it!

Thursday 4th

Went up to Miss Potting in the playground and apologized for my 'appalling behaviour' at the rehearsal. I said I had only been trying something new to impress her because I thought she was the greatest director since Francis Ford Coppola. I said that her direction was an inspiration to me, and that when I grew up to be a great actor I would never forget

that I owed it all to her, if only she would give me another chance. It was a tear-jerking performance that only the hardest-hearted person in the universe could have resisted. Miss Potting just glared at me and told me to get lost. She is even harder-hearted than I thought, or there's something wrong with her.

Friday 5th

Stayed in bed today because I didn't feel like going to school and have Amanda Lucey make fun of

me. Spent the day racking my brains to come up with a scheme to get myself back in the school play, and also get my own back on that Lucey, the slimeball.

Sunday 7th

Yesterday I spent the day cutting out newspaper accounts of accidents and, using the photocopier down at the library, I produced what looked like a glossy colour supplement called: 'Your Holiday Special: Accidents at Historical Sites in Britain'. This morning I slipped it into the Sunday paper when it arrived. The paper already has about fifteen parts to it, so one more part wasn't suspicious. Dad started reading it and gradually his face turned pale. My guess was he'd come to the bit about people being beheaded by Roman remains falling on them from a great height and other people dying of blood poisoning after accidentally treading on Stone Age axes. He passed it across to Mum and her face turned white, too.

Meanwhile, I began to read aloud from the real holiday section, in particular the bit about Safe Family Holidays by the Sea.

Monday 8th

I have found out why Miss Potting is so sour! She's fallen for the new History teacher, Mr Kunzle, but she's so shy she can't bring herself to even talk to him!

What's made her even more unhappy is he doesn't even seem notice her! This will be my Secret Weapon!

Tuesday 9th

Began my Get-Me-Back-In-the-Play Campaign today. Made sure I was standing just outside the staff room door as Miss Potting came out at break, and said to my pal Irons, 'Mr Kunzle gave me an A for my History project! He said I'm his best student. Not bad, eh?' Then I wandered off, dragging Irons with me before he could open his mouth and say, 'But you don't have Mr Kunzle for History!'

That afternoon Miss Potting stopped me as I was walking across the playground and said, pretending to be casual, 'How do you get on with that new teacher. Mr What's-his-name ... Kunzle?'

Just in case it was a trick question I played it careful, just gave a cautious smile and said, 'It would be wrong of me give an opinion about a teacher to another teacher, even though I have to say I think he's great.' As she was taking this in, I added, 'That's a bit of a coincidence, though, because he was asking me the same about you yesterday.'

Just then the bell went for the start of lessons and I scooted off, leaving her open-mouthed and looking like she was going to have a panic attack.

After school I saw Miss Potting hanging around by the front gate, trying to appear casual again, but obviously looking for me so she could find out what Mr Kunzle and I had said about her. I decided to make her sweat about it over night, so I sneaked out through the back gate.

Wednesday 10th

Miss Potting must have been waiting outside the school all night, because when I arrived this morning she was there. Before she could open her mouth I moved in first, saying, 'Miss Potting, I was just coming to see you!'

'Yes?!' she said eagerly.

'About the school play,' I said, and her face fell.

'Oh that!' she snapped, and then she stopped as she realized that the key to her future happiness with Mr Kunzle depended on her getting the low-down about the idiot from me. And that depended on her getting in my good books. She huffed and puffed and stomped around the pavement a bit, then she said, through gritted teeth, 'Actually, I was going to talk to you about that today. About, you know, giving you your part back.'

I made my eyes light up with delight and surprise at this 'unexpected' news and said, 'Cor! Really, Miss Potting! Thanks! I'll be at rehearsal at lunch time.' I then added, 'Mr Kunzle will be really pleased.'

Her face turned a deep pink. 'He will?' she said. 'Why?'

'Because he told me he thought I had great acting talent.'

'He did?!' squeaked Miss Potting.

'He did,' I said. 'He also said he had doubts about Amanda Lucey as an actress, but then History's his subject, not Drama, so what does he know?' With that I gave a light laugh and zoomed off into school before she could ask me anything else about Kunzle and his views on acting.

Thursday 11th

Rehearsal at lunch time. Amanda Lucey got one line wrong and Miss Potting gave her a blasting, said she was useless and if she didn't buck up her ideas she'd be lucky to play the part of the camel's hump in *Lawrence of Arabia*.

Me, on the other hand, I forgot nearly all my lines, and Miss Potting praised me for my 'inspirational improvisational performance'. Amanda Lucey nearly burst two blood vessels with anger.

Friday 12th

Dad came home with a stack of brochures about seaside holidays. Although nothing has been said, I think I may have won this one. Decided to give my powerful brain a well-deserved rest over the weekend.

Monday 15th

AAAARGHHHH!!!! TRAGEDY!! DISASTER!!! As I was leaving school I overheard Miss Potting telling Mrs Wilson that she is going to ask Mr Kunzle to help with the school play because she thinks he might be 'interested in drama'.

This is a nightmare! My whole plan was based on the fact that Potting was too shy to actually TALK to Kunzle. If they actually exchange words, I'm sunk! Drastic measures are called for!

Tuesday 16th

Spent last night talking to kids in Kunzle's class to try to find out his weak spot, and found out that he is mad keen on being promoted. So, I went to school early this morning so I could see Mr Kunzle before Miss Potting got to him. As he got out of his car I rushed up to him and said, 'Mr Kunzle, sir! Could I talk to you a moment about the school play...?!'

Instead of looking interested, he scowled (which I've noticed teachers seem to do a lot lately) and snapped, 'I'm not interested in drama.'

Things were looking bad, but thinking quickly, as he was about to walk off I said, 'Oh, that's a pity, sir, because I heard the Head say he was thinking of giving promotion to the teachers who help with the school play, and because I think you're such a good teacher, I thought I'd let you know that.'

This stopped him in his tracks. He came back and said, 'When did you hear the Head say this?'

'Yesterday,' I said. 'He said it to Mrs King, the School Secretary, but it's supposed to be a secret. At the moment Miss Potting is the only one who does the school play, so I suppose she'll get the promotion.'

'What promotion is that?' asked

Kunzle, his eyes narrowing greedily.

'I didn't hear that part,' I said, 'only that there's going to be a promotion.' I bowed my head apologetically. 'I'm sorry, sir, I shouldn't have said all that. I know it's wrong to pass on other people's conversations...'

'Yes it is,' said Kunzle. 'And don't you forget it. However, I'll let you off this time ... if you keep your mouth shut in future.'

With that, he headed for the school buildings, and I could tell by the way he walked he was already thinking in terms of Mr Kunzle, Head of Department.

Wednesday 17th

Surprise surprise! Mr Kunzle came to Miss Potting and offered to help her with the school play! Miss Potting was highly delighted, she went all pink around the face and said it would be her pleasure, and then spent the whole of the rehearsal gazing at him, while he spent the rehearsal picking his nose. As he told me yesterday, he's got no interest in drama. All I have to do now is make sure that Amanda Lucey screws up at the actual performance on Friday night, so I get a bigger round of applause than her.

Thursday 18th

Amanda Lucey was really nervous and got told off by both Miss Potting and Mr Kunzle. She went off in tears. Things are looking good for me for tomorrow.

Friday 19th

AAARGHHH!!!! That fiend in human shape, that pile of dog's dropping, that boil, Amanda Lucey beat me and won the bet! My plan went perfectly. On stage I was brilliant (well, better than her, anyway) but when it came to the crunch, the part where you go out on stage after the end of the play and the audience cheer and clap, that rotten hideous vampire locked me in the toilet so I couldn't get on stage! So, even though only two people clapped her (her mum and dad) she won!

Then, to cap it all, when I did manage to get out of the toilet who should I hear but Miss Potting and Mr Kunzle, with him saying, 'No I won't have time to help with your next production because I won't have a lot of time to spare, what with my promotion, plus the fact that my wife and four children don't see much of me at the moment anyway.'

It was the way Miss Potting's voice went up and out of the range of human hearing at the word 'wife' that made me think it would be a good idea if I made my exit. I was just trying to sneak past them, doing my best to look invisible, when Miss Potting brought her voice back within human range again and snapped 'Then why did you ask about me?!'

'Who said I asked about you?' said Kunzle, looking baffled.

Just then Miss Potting saw me. Thinking quickly I said, 'Where am I? Where is this? Who am I?'

As they gawped at me, I managed to stumble past them, and then rushed off as fast as I could to where my mum and dad were waiting for me.

'There you are,' said Mum. 'We waited for you to come out on stage so we could clap, but you never appeared.'

'I got stuck in the toilet,' I said.

'Oh dear,' said Dad. 'Never mind, we've got some news that'll cheer you up. Because of the interest you've shown in going on a History Holiday, bringing home that video tape and everything, we've put you down to go on one with your History teacher, Mr Kunzle, while me and your mum go for a boring old break by the seaside. With Mr Kunzle looking after you you'll be able to enjoy yourself in safety.'

'And it'll be even doubly brilliant fun for you,' said Mum cheerfully, 'because we hear your favourite Drama teacher, Miss Potting, is going on it as well!'

OTHER HILARIOUS BOOKS FROM RED FOX

RICKY'S THESAURUS
A DIRTY DAY IN THE PARK

WILL WELCH AND CLIVE COLLINS

When Ricky opens his thesaurus he knows he going to get some wordy help from a very unusual source – his pal, Thes, a genuine, real, *bona fide* prehistoric dinosaur.

So when life hits a high in the dull-stakes who better to accompany him to the park for a bit of excitement. But Mum's, 'Don't get dirty, Ricky,' warning is still ringing in his ears as he encounters a number of tricky, sticky and ultimately mucky situations. It's lucky he's got Thes on hand to stop things turning into a complete catastrophe, calamity or even disaster!

Crazy capers from comic strip characters with real appeal!

ISBN - 0 09 955951 X £2.99

OTHER HILARIOUS BOOKS FROM RED FOX

RICKY'S THESAURUS
TESTING TIMES

WILL WELCH AND CLIVE COLLINS

Once again Ricky opens his thesaurus and out pops Thes, his prehistoric pal with a talent for talking, the gift of the gab and a really rather wonderful way with words!

It's exam time for Ricky and one thing's for sure, he's not looking forward to them at all, one bit, or even very slightly. As Ricky bluffs his way through art and chemistry he's only glad Thes is on hand for moral support in English. But Ricky's got some hidden talents and with a little help from Thes he's sure to come out top of the class!

Crazy capers from comic strip characters with real appeal!

ISBN - 0 09 955951 X £2.99

BULLYBUSTER'S JOKE BOOK

JOHN BYRNE

'School Bully thinks he's hard...'
'He is now - we just poured cement over him!'

Hundreds of hilarious put-downs for the lowest of the low - bullies. Bullies may think they're smart but they're not, and this collection of fantastically funny jokes and back-answers will give your anti-bullying strategy a seriously funny start.

Packed with laughs, there's also a serious side with plenty of tips, advice and useful phone numbers to help you put every sort of bully in their place.

Witty ways to knock bullies for six!

ISBN - O O9 960981 9 £2.50